MYSTIC MICHIGAN
PART FOUR
IV

by
Mark Jager

ZOSMA PUBLICATIONS

P.O. Box 284
Marion, Michigan 49665
www.zosmapublications.com

MYSTIC MICHIGAN
PART FOUR
by Mark Jager

•

Published by
ZOSMA PUBLICATIONS
P.O. Box 284
Marion, Michigan 49665
(231)743-6984

•

Maps throughout this book are courtesy of the
Michigan Department of Transportation

•

Design and layout by Deana Jager

•

Editing by Brenda Hamacher

•

*Story # **23~Will-o'-wisps of Michigan** is
contributed by Dan Wood of Three Rivers, MI

ISBN   0-9672464-6-6

3 4 5 6 7 8 9 / 05 04 03 02

DEDICATED TO

This book is dedicated to the memory of my father, Les Jager, who
always encouraged me, supported me, loved me and
showed an interest in what I was doing.
I'll always love him and he is greatly missed.

TABLE OF CONTENTS

1~Ruins of Michigan's Lost City

Through a myriad of dancing branches and leaves and the interplay of sunshine and shadow it creates on the forest floor, you see in the distance what appears to be the vast ruins of an ancient lost city. "Could this be?" you ask yourself. You are in a woodland area near Baldwin, Michigan.

As you continue your journey, your eyes fall upon massive formations that assume the likeness of ancient Roman archways and aqueducts. Some of the archways are 30 feet tall. A quick glance around you reveals long-forgotten walls which run for dozens if not hundreds of feet. Some of these walls are three feet thick and 30 or more feet tall.

As the wind whispers its ancient song through the poplar and sassafras trees, you see enormous caverns. These coves look like they were once lined with bricks. You also see huge basement areas. They are all that remain of titanic buildings which once stood in this location. You stare in amazement as you realize that the basement alone is massive. Although many years of forest growth has come up through the basement floor and trees now tower 30 feet high inside the basement, you can still see the outline of it. It's bigger than a football field!

As you make your way through this huge basement, you see what looks like a tunnel. You walk up to it and see that it's filled with water. The end of it is nowhere in sight. You look behind you, and there lies the entrance to still another tunnel. This one is not filled with water, so you start making your way through it. After walking quite a number of feet, you emerge from a subterranean chamber in a different location. You have traveled a considerable distance underground!

You look off through the forest and see that what you have mistaken for several huge trees are actually tall cement towers that look almost like obelisks. That's not all. You have to watch your steps because there are booby traps at different places in this forgotten city. There are holes in the ground that drop down 20 feet into areas with concrete floors. All throughout the woods you can see cement structures hidden and obscured by the trees of the wilderness. How many hidden tunnels, towers, and structures are there out here? What are they doing in Michigan? Is this for real or are you just dreaming?

Believe it or not, such a place does actually exist in Michigan. It is one of Michigan's best kept secrets. It is located on private property near Baldwin. The ruins are literally what's left of the Michigan ghost town of Marlboro, which can still be located on old Michigan maps. The town had nearly 70 homes at one time. The massive cement structures were built nearly 100 years ago, and placed in various locations by the town's cement company. The ruins are on private property now, and cannot be entered without the permission of the owner. For more information, contact the Baldwin Historical Society.

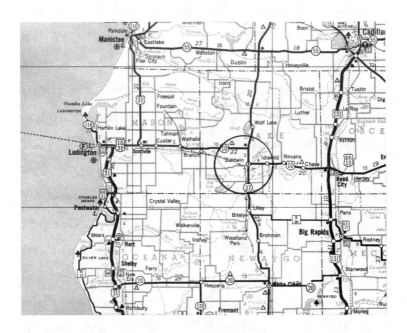

2~Michigan's Mystic Tower

A Michigan light tower appears to some people to be beckoning from the great beyond. It seems to be twinkling out its ghostly code to mariners on the inland sea of Lake Huron.

The Presque Isle lighthouse has been shocking observers for several years now. This is because a number of people claim that they have seen the lighthouse doing something that can't be scientifically explained.

According to a story that appeared on the front page of the Bay City Times (Oct. 27, 2000), the lighthouse is exhibiting a strange light at the top of its tower. This wouldn't be so unusual if it weren't for the fact that all of the electricity has been disconnected from the tower for nearly three decades.

According to the Bay City Times, in June of 1979, the lighthouse keeper, George Parris, and a Coast Guard officer disconnected all of the electrical wires, and removed all of the gears, switches and the bulb. In spite of this, visiting boaters and fishermen as well as many local residents have reported seeing a glowing amber light at the top of the lighthouse.

The <u>Times</u> reported that the odd light appears nightly. Some people think that the mysterious light is simply reflected light from the moon or passing boats. The widow of the old lighthouse keeper publically announced that she believes that the bizarre glow is the spirit of her late husband beckoning the townspeople.

Whatever the explanation is for the light, there are many people who have claimed to have observed it. <u>Bay City Times</u> photographer Rick Gillard and reporter Kathie Marchlewski claim to have witnessed this phenomenon firsthand while investigating the tower for their newspaper.

3~The Michigan Mermaid

In 1950, Sammy of Sammy's Gifts and Gallery in East Tawas Michigan ordered a life size mermaid to display out in front of her shoreline gift store. The mermaid became an attraction to tourists. People had their pictures taken with it. It seemed to help business. What Sammy didn't realize is that the mermaid would be involved in an odd set of circumstances.

Sammy gave the mermaid away to a fellow business owner who wanted to use it for his Michigan business. After doing this, she realized that the mermaids were no longer available for ordering. Many years went by, and many people wondered what had happened to the mermaid. Sammy wished she could get another one, but couldn't find one anywhere.

Sammy had given up on trying to order a

substitute mermaid because it seemed as if they were no longer available. Years after she had given up hope, she received a message from a friend out in California. Her friend informed her that they had found a substitute mermaid in a secondhand store out on the west coast.

Needless to say, after all of those years Sammy was happy to finally get a substitute mermaid. Upon receiving the figure, she decided it needed more stuffing. As she was stuffing it, her hand struck something hard. She reached in and pulled out a carved wooden spoon. It was the very spoon she had put in the mermaid many years before. Her mermaid had, under strange circumstances, come back to her after all of those years. How the mermaid got back to Tawas has forever remained a mystery to Sammy.

4~Michigan: A Massive Ancient Cemetery

According to reports, in 1890 James O. Scotford of Edmore, Michigan, was hired to erect a fence around a cattle range in Montcalm County for James Remick. While building the fence, the line ran across a small hill about 30 feet across.

While digging a hole for a fence post, the post hole digger struck something hard. Prompted by curiosity, he dug the object up, and to his utter amazement he found it to be a large earthen casket.

He took the casket to Edmore Michigan and showed it to the townspeople. He also showed it to the citizens of Wyman, a village 3 miles away. Excitement filled the town. Many of the villagers searched the forests and found numerous small mounds and hills.

Before too long, villagers had gone

around the area and opened up between 400 to 500 mounds and discovered approximately 100 cists, or small boxes. Many other artifacts were found including clay tablets. Some of the relics are reported to have been beautifully carved with ancient Bible scenes, historic scenes, symbols and writing.

A man named M.E. Cornell wrote a book which described the discoveries of the people of Montcalm County. Cornell described the mounds' contents in the following way. "Many curious things were unearthed, such as caskets, tablets, amulets of slate stone, cups, vases, altars, lamps of burnt clay, copper coins hammered out and rudely engraved with hieroglyphics. The cists are of sun-dried clay, and are covered with picture writing and hieroglyphics. The cists seem to be intended as receptacles for the tablets of record. They have close-fitting covers, which are cemented on with Assyrian-like cement, and various figures were molded on the top: the ancient sphinx, beasts, serpents, human faces with headdresses or crowns, etc."

In 1907, Daniel E. Soper, who at one time was Michigan's Secretary of State, became interested in Michigan's prehistoric race of people. In G. Major Tabors' book Prehistoric Man Tabors wrote the following report of Secretary of State Soper's archaeological find. "By personal effort he (Soper) opened up 117 mounds, some of them within a ten-mile radius of Detroit. In several mounds he found 14 clay pipes, no two alike, and on a stone tablet there is displayed representations of Adam and Eve, the Flood, Noah's Ark with the dove seeking dry land, and animals leaving the ark, besides the temple of sun worshipers."

According to reports, on March 1, 1916, an article appeared in the Chattanooga News in Tennessee. Soper had moved to Tennessee. The article stated that Soper had been in Michigan for nine years. He had dug in various mounds of the ancient mound builders. He had collected hundreds of remarkable relics of the mysterious race which once inhabited Michigan and the Great Lakes Basin of North America.

According to literature, on September 18, 1916, the <u>Washington Post</u> reported "Prehistoric tablets of great value found by Dr. Hyvernat in Michigan." The article stated that, "On September 12, Dr. Henri Hyvernat of the Catholic University of Washington, D.C. took from a mound in the woods north of Detroit a slate tablet about a foot long with a circular calendar engraved on one side."

Another man from Detroit, the Reverend James Savage, also excavated relics. Savage was quoted as saying, "We are confident that we are only on the borderland of the great prehistoric people."

In 1817, Mr. Brickenridge, a historian of Jackson County, wrote, "The great number and extremely large size of some of them (cities) may be regarded as furnishing, with other circumstances, evidences of antiquity. I have sometimes been induced to think that at the period when they were constructed, there was population here (in Michigan) as big as that which once animated the borders of the Nile or Euphrates or of Mexico. I am perfectly satisfied that cities similar to those of ancient Mexico of several thousand souls have existed in this country." (<u>History of Jackson County</u>, Brickenridge, Page 20)

Do the caskets and burial mounds of Michigan have something to do with this ancient civilization? According to literature, on August 26, 1911, an article appeared in a Detroit newspaper. The article stated that it was believed that a large portion of the entire state of Michigan was a great ancient burial ground. It is reported that by 1911 so many mounds had been opened in Michigan that it appeared as if a large portion of the entire state was nothing more than a titanic ancient cemetery. Mr. John Russell, one of the researchers, stated that he believed that the old cemetery stretched all the way from Jackson County through Washtenaw County and into Wayne. Thousands of mounds were opened and explored. Some pilgrims knew that these mounds were not Indian mounds. They wondered whose descendants they were, Shem, Ham, or Japeth's. As late as 1977 groups were still coming to Michigan to look for the relics of the ancient civilization. (See Escanaba Daily Press, Tuesday, Dec. 27, 1977)

Although many of these artifacts can still be seen around the country, there is still controversy surrounding their authenticity. The Detroit News published articles in the early 1900s claiming that counterfeiters forged many of the relics. There were also many archaeologists who claimed that nearly all of the relics were just a deception. They claimed that all of the 22,000 tablets were planted by pranksters throughout the state. It is rumored that the relics have never even been carbon dated. The mounds of Michigan are a reality and the objects taken out of them really do exist. Whether a person believes the artifacts were placed there by an ancient civilization or by pranksters all depends on which "experts" one chooses to believe.

5~Michigan 1999 Fireball Phenomenon

On November 16, 1999, blue-green-orange fireballs began raining down over the skies of Northern Michigan. At 7:11 p.m. the phones at the Wexford County law enforcement agencies began ringing. Various people witnessed the rain of fireballs.

According to a front-page article published by the Cadillac Evening News on Nov. 17, 1999, Emily Roncari of Tustin saw an oval-shaped light moving in the southern skies. "To me it looked like one big sphere. As it went to the east, it looked like it broke up into five different pieces." Emily Roncari's father, Ed Roncari, saw the objects for several seconds. In his opinion, the objects looked like flying machines. "We saw crafts," he said. "There were four of them, all in line with each other. They moved noiselessly, low, tree-top height, but in the distance. Do you know how jet liners have signal lights always blinking? This was a straight line, not blinking. They were tan-yellow as I saw them. I've seen shooting stars. They're fast, this was slow."

Sheriff's departments in Wexford, Lake, and Grand Traverse Counties received many calls during the event.

6~Michigan's Subterranean Worlds

Far beneath our feet is an incredible Michigan underground world. There are a variety of different places all throughout Michigan which contain miles of caverns that remain virtually unknown to most Michiganders.

Did you know that there are vast subterranean areas underneath the city of Grand Rapids? Old gypsum mines have been converted into storage areas. Large semis actually drive down underground roads to subterranean warehouses to pick up goods. There are people who actually work underground. There are nearly 6 miles of underground tunnels in Grand Rapids just at one business alone. The Michigan Natural Storage Company is 80 feet underground. Food, micro-film, and computer records are stored at the underground warehouse.

The underground storage company covers 45,000 square feet. The company conducts group tours. Domtar Corporation operates an underground gypsum business 100 feet beneath Butterworth Avenue, and there is another mine near the Kent County Airport.

The city of Detroit is known for its salt mines. One of the best known is the Detroit Salt Mine. In order to reach the mines you have to descend 1,400 feet. There are over 100 miles of tunnels at the business. The mine spreads out over 1,500 acres. (For pictures see www.detroitsalt.com)

There are also large caverns in the Upper Peninsula. One of the best known is the iron mine at Iron Mountain, Michigan. At the mine, people can ride a small train into the earth. Underneath the adjoining Michigan cities of Negaunee and Ishpeming there are nearly 180 miles of abandoned mines. There are such vast caverns underneath Negaunee that huge sections of the town have literally caved in.

There are also other smaller underground

areas underneath Michigan cities. One such place is underneath Cadillac. There are underground passages in the older section of town which lead to many different downtown businesses. The passageways were used to bring coal to the establishments years ago. There may be many such passages beneath many Michigan cities.

7~The Hemlock Lights

A strange and unusual light phenomenon was often seen in the forest regions between Hemlock and Merrill, Michigan, from the mid 1960s through the early 1980s.

"The lights were fog or something like it," said Vicki Buckley of Merrill. "The fog-like formation was illuminated. It would actually float and move around. There were some areas that were brighter than others. The fog emitted a very dull glow. You couldn't explain where it came from. It would grow brighter and dimmer. It never really did get that bright."

Buckley mentioned that the Hemlock lights were quite popular in the 1960s. At that time there was an old barn out in that area that an old man had committed suicide in. Since the early 1980s many homes have been built in the area. Buckley mentioned that she hasn't heard as much about the lights in recent years.

However, it is still a possibility that the eerie illuminated fog may still be seen in certain areas.

Vicki Buckley's brother-in-law also commented on the gas. "It did happen in my time era," he said. "Many people figured it was the moon or stars shining on swamp gas." One woman who was in the area many years ago commented on her encounter. "I was sitting down at the end of a dirt trail. The light became greater and brighter. It got so bright that it lit up the whole inside of the dash, then it vanished," she said. The lights were often seen off M-46 near Steel Road.

8~Michigan Treasure Island Hermit

A mysterious hermit once lived on a small 30-acre island now called Treasure Island off of Point Comfort on the southwest side of Higgins Lake.

For a large number of years before 1900, a man named Israel Porter Pritchard settled on the island. People called him the hermit of Higgins Lake. There are some who say that the old man went into hiding following the accidental death of his wife who many believed he had murdered.

The hermit occupied a small cabin for many years, and then vanished. His cabin was found vacant when campers investigated it one summer. In 1929, Lloyd L. Harman of Higgins Lake said that several years after the hermit had disappeared he returned to find that his cabin had been burnt down. In the summer of either

1902 or 1903, his corpse was found and removed from the island by authorities. Even to this day the hermit is occasionally thought of and mentioned. There are various strange stories throughout Michigan of odd island dwellers.

9~Strange Animal Encounters in Michigan

Sometimes Michiganders see things that surprise them and have no logical explanation.

On September 23,1984, a female motorist reported to Detroit authorities that she had seen a kangaroo hop across I-94 near the Detroit Metropolitan Airport. A kangaroo was also reported by sheriff's deputies the next day. The strange thing is, the creature was never found.

In May of 1984 a large black panther was witnessed lurking in the residential areas of Manchester, Michigan. In August of the same year there were five sightings of a black panther near the Fisher Body Plant in Flint, Michigan.

According to a book called Curious Encounters, a strange encounter took place in Saginaw in 1937. A resident reported that he had seen a man-like water creature climb up a river bank, lean against a tree, and then jump back into the water. The person who had seen the creature is reported to have had a nervous breakdown.

In addition to this, the D.N.R. gets 10 to 12 calls each year from people who think they have seen Michigan mountain lions. Mountain lions were historically found in Michigan.

10~Lake Erie's Fairy Grotto

An incredible island with magical caves filled with brilliant sparkling gemstones lies in the mysterious waters of Lake Erie southeast of Detroit.

South Bass Island is the home of 20 spectacular caves. Two of the caves, Crystal Cave and Perry's Cave, contain fascinating features and are open for public viewing. Crystal Cave has celestite in it. Celestite is a white mineral containing strontium. In the cavern, water mineralized with celestite creating gem-like formations. Some of the crystals from the cave are now on display at the Smithsonian Institute in Washington. D.C. The cave is beautiful and has earned the nickname of "The Fairy Grotto." A cave guide once claimed that many people have come to the cave in order to place coins in the caves' wishing well.

The other main cave, Perry's Cave, also has interesting features. The two caves have been open for public viewing since the late 1800s.

In the past, colored lights were placed in the cave to highlight the gemstone features.

The island is captivating and was at one time the home of a tremendous palace/hotel with over 600 rooms. Even in the modern day there are some dazzling structures on the island. There are a couple of interesting stone-pillared Greek-styled buildings on the island, and in between them stands the third tallest national monument in the United States, Perry's International Peace and Victory Monument. The monument commemorates the American victory over the British during the battle of Lake Erie.

The monument is made out of 80,000 cubic feet of pink granite. It was built from 1912 to 1915 and towers 352 feet above the island. The monument is capped with an 11-ton bronze urn. In addition to these interesting features, there are also vineyards on the island, as well as three museums and the world's longest restaurant bar. Perry's Cave can be contacted at 419-285-2405, Crystal Cave at 419-285-2811.

11~Michigan's Underwater Forest

Researchers from the University of Colorado's Institute for Research in Environmental Sciences have claimed to discover that Lake Erie was subjected to a cataclysmic flood several thousand years ago which caused the lake to spill out of its borders. The flood is reported to have swallowed up enormous forest lands near Detroit, southeast Michigan, and Ontario, Canada, creating a huge underwater forest. The flood also buried human settlements and is believed by some researchers to be responsible for causing the modern version of Niagara Falls.

The Colorado University research team, headed by Troy Holcomb, studied several hundred thousand soundings of the lake to determine the geography of the lake's bottom. The soundings were taken by such organizations as the U.S. Army Corps of Engineers, The Canadian Hydrographic Service, and the U.S. National Oceanic and

Atmospheric Administration.

Researchers studying the sounding of the lake bottom discovered a large number of sandbars, ridges, and river deltas on the lake bottom. Researchers believe that several thousand years ago, Lake Erie's water/shoreline levels were between 33 and 50 feet lower than the shoreline water levels are at the present time.

Researcher Troy Holcomb said, "All around the lake you have these features that look like shoreline features that are in the range of 33 to 55 feet deep." Holcomb believes that before the catastrophic flood the western basin of Lake Erie was dry land, and he believes that it was possible to walk from places in southern Ontario, such as Point Pelee, to the south-eastern corner of Michigan and northern Ohio. He also believes that Lake Erie was an inland sea whose level was maintained by rivers flowing into it, along with precipitation and evaporation. He stated that at one time there was not a channel flowing into Lake Erie from Lake Huron. He suggests that water drained from the three upper Great Lakes into outlets near North Bay and down the Ottawa River.

Holcomb believes the Ottawa River outlets

became blocked. When this happened, the water levels in the upper lakes began to rise like a bathtub with the taps turned on, until the water levels rose high enough to spill out into Lake Erie. Holcomb believes that one of the consequences of the flood was that Erie began draining out of the Niagara River which caused the re-creation of Niagara Falls. It is believed that before this time, Niagara Falls had fallen silent during a several thousand year period of low water levels. The rise in water levels is thought to have left a gigantic underwater forest, and is also believed to have submerged any ancient settlements or civilizations that may have existed at that time. More information on this topic may be found on the Internet from the Toronto Globe newspaper in an article by Martin Mittelstaedt.

12~Michigan Circle and Square

When explorers first came to a place which would later become known as the city of Tecumseh, Michigan, they found a very strange formation,

Near the bank of the river Raisen, at a place once known as Brownsville, was a structure made of earth. Accurate descriptions of this construction have been left by pioneers of the region.

The earthen structure was in the form of a circle joined by a passageway to a square. According to Hinsdale's Archaeological Atlas of Michigan, 200 years ago there were still remains of cedar posts standing which seemed to indicate that at one time the embankments were palisaded. It is reported that in the center of the circle there were a number of pits. Not far from the circle and the square were two other circular enclosures. The purpose of the structure is unknown. There are various theories concerning the circle and the square and similar earth designs that have been found in Michigan. (See Mystic Michigan Part One)

13~The Lights Of Michigan's Denton Road

There have been many people who have reported that there is a strange light phenomenon that occurs in Canton Township, Michigan.

The strange light is said to be seen near a bridge that goes over the branch of the lower Rouge River, on Denton Road. For years people have claimed to see a glowing ball of light near the bridge. One former Canton resident said, "We were driving down Denton Road and we saw a light that appeared to follow our car down the road. I believe the light exists. There are other people I know who claim that the light actually came down and burnt their car."

Local people have called the light "the blue lady" over the years. Legends have surfaced about the light, making strange claims about it. Others believe that the light is nothing more than a hoax, put on by local teens. Virginia Bailey Parker wrote about the light in a book called <u>Ghost Stories and Other Tales From Canton</u> (The Canton Historical Society).

Sharon Le Dillenbeck of Canton spoke of an experience her daughter reported having in a car with some of her friends on Denton Road in 1997. It was reported in an October 1999 issue of the <u>Detroit Free Press</u>. Dillenbeck's daughter said the car started going faster at the bridge for no apparent reason. The <u>Detroit Press</u> claims that there were articles printed on the light by the now defunct newspaper <u>The Ypsilanti Press</u>.

This odd phenomenon has not been scientifically verified. If you are an eyewitness of this natural oddity we would like to hear your story.

42

14~Michigan's Reappearing Historic Ship

The hull of a 119-year-old ship named the "Minnehana" can still be seen from time to time just off the shore of Arcadia, Michigan.

In November of 1999 the waters of the Great Lakes were dropping due to a lack of rain. Arcadia residents who made their way down to the beach were surprised to see that the hull of the 200 foot sunken schooner had appeared along the shore.

It was not the first time the hull of the ship has been seen. The last time the ship's hull was seen was in the 1930s when water levels dropped. The four masted Minnehana sunk in the fall of 1893 while carrying 58,000 bushels of corn on its way from Chicago to Point Edward, Ontario.

As water levels rise, the Minnehana

disappears. When the water levels go back down it appears again. Years pass between appearances, sometimes decades. However, when the time is right the Minnehana reappears to relay to the living its timeless message of the perils of the inland seas. For more information see the November 29, 1999, front page article that appeared in the <u>Traverse City Record Eagle</u>.

15~Michigan's Forest Cemeteries

There are a number of cemeteries that are located in highly unusual places in Michigan. One such cemetery is the old Walton Junction cemetery.

The Walton Junction cemetery is a graveyard that contains the dead of a once thriving lumber town. Most of the corpses in the cemetery were born in the 1800s. After the lumbermen left the town, its buildings fell into ruins and disappeared. Now all that remains is the cemetery.

The cemetery is found in an unsuspecting place, right out in the middle of the woods. After traveling down a two-track one can find the forgotten cemetery by following a small footpath. The old graveyard is surrounded by rocks which mark its perimeter. There are remains of cemeteries in even stranger places in

Michigan.

The cemetery in Cadillac was actually moved across town at one time. The old cemetery was located on Evart Street near Mercy Hospital. Years after the caskets were dug up and taken to Maple Hill cemetery, people digging foundations for homes were still finding bones.

16~Michigan's Lost Gold Mine

There was a gold rush in Michigan in the late 1800s. There were several well-known gold mines in the Upper Peninsula. Ropes Mine was open as late as 1989 (see <u>Mystic Michigan Part 1</u>). However, there was a gold mine open in the Lower Peninsula too. The strange thing about this Lower Peninsula gold mine is that it has vanished in the mists of time, and has become Michigan's lost gold mine.

In November of 1912, gold was discovered on the Flemming farm near Harrisville, in Haynes Township, Alcona County. In 1913 a mine shaft was sunk to a depth of nearly 100 feet. Nearly a year after this, there was an explosion in the mine. The four Dome brothers who did the mining were killed. The mine shaft proceeded to be filled with water. As of 1971, the site of the mine had never been located. This is the last report we have heard about the mine.

Frank Jozwiak of Harrison at one time owned the property the mine was located on. Jozwiak says his father told him a story of an old man who lived in a shack near the mine. The old man snuck down to the river's edge while everyone else was involved in sinking a mine shaft. He worked during the summer hauling dirt to his property. He spent all winter panning for gold. Jozwiak said the old man made his living off the gold for years.

17~Michigan's Underwater Metropolis

According to at least two different publications, mysterious stone structures built by an ancient civilization have been discovered by divers in the bottom of Lake Erie.

According to the Australian Magazine Breakthroughs, scientists studying changes in the bottom of Lake Erie have discovered stone structures in the north central regions of Lake Erie in 260 feet of water. A report in the Weekly World News states that a team of scientists headed by Australian archaeologist Dr. Anthony Berens have found what appears to be an ancient metropolis.

"We've got sonar readings that clearly reveal a carefully laid out urban area, complete with two large temples or public buildings, a central park like area and several wide boulevards," Dr. Berens is quoted as saying.

Reporter Lisa Merakis of the <u>World News</u> claims that paved streets and a public stadium, as well as fountains and temples have been found. Berens is quoted by the <u>World News</u> as saying that underwater photographs reveal deep clefts and rifts in the streets and walls which indicate that the city was struck by a powerful earthquake before it sank. The same report says that divers have discovered artifacts that date back as far as 1,500 B.C. and that Dr.Berens has been working with a team of U.S. marine specialists in a federally funded survey of the Great Lakes basins.

Anyone with more information on the validity of this story is encouraged to send it to Zosma Publications. This article is only reporting the claims of various reporters. At this point this is only a rumor and cannot be stated as an absolute fact until we get updated and verified information on it.

18~Medieval Michigan

Did you know that there are areas in Michigan that resemble the places and times of the Middle Ages?

There are actually huge Renaissance festivals in Michigan. People come to them dressed in Middle Age clothing to attend Medieval events. One such festival is in Holly, Michigan. Lowell and Carey Godfrey of Newaygo go to the Renaissance festival every year. Lowell Godfrey commented, "At the festival they have full contact jousting and axe and star throwing. There is also a live theater. In addition there are over 50 merchants on hand. You can buy everything from Middle Age weapons to clothing to food. The festival serves huge feasts with 12 to 15 courses. There are minstrels providing music, and Viking storytellers providing entertainment."

There are also a number of castles which can be observed in Michigan. One of the biggest is located near Canadian Lakes, Michigan. The castle is quite large and looks like an authentic Middle Age castle with the exception of satellite dishes sticking off the side of it. The grounds around the castle are pleasant. There is a large patio on the back of the castle where guests can sit and enjoy themselves.

To relax near the castle can actually bring one into a medieval state of mind. At times there are actually plays and banquets held at the castle. The Canadian Lakes castle is not the only one in Michigan. There are a number of castles elsewhere. One of them is Curwood Castle in Owosso. The castle was built from 1922 to 1923 by author James Oliver Curwood. Curwood wrote several of his novels there.

Perhaps the most well-known castle in Michigan is Castle Farms Theater in Charlevoix. The castle was built by Albert and Anna Loeb in 1918. The castle is a replica of a French country estate. Another castle is Bennett Castle in Ypsilanti. It was built by

Henry Ford's right-hand man, Harry Bennett, in 1929. Bennett's castle was built to protect him from enemies he had made while he was head of security at Ford Motor Company. Bennett's castle has lion and tiger dens, secret doors, tunnels and escape routes as well as two huge gun towers.

19~Michigan Explosion Oddity

An Ohio man visiting Michigan claims to have witnessed a strange explosion phenomenon. Jack Stephens, 77, was fishing alone on Weatherhog Lake in the Upper Peninsula when the event took place.

"One muggy September evening at around 6 :00 or 7:00 p.m. I was out fishing by myself. Suddenly I heard crackles going off in the distance," Stephens said. "The crackles started out slowly, comparable in speed and intensity to what you would expect to hear if it started raining lightly; a drop here, a drop there. Except the sound I was hearing was not the sound of raindrops, but a sound which was similar to a shotgun being fired."

"Some of the sounds were close by, others were far away. I could hear them exploding randomly. Then, similar in progression to a pattern of going from light rain to a heavy downpour, the explosions started increasing in speed and in intensity and were everywhere around me. The explosions built up to a peak and then suddenly stopped. These things were just going off everywhere. This really happened."

"For a while I thought it may have had something to do with the B-52 bombers that often flew over the lake. There weren't any planes nearby and there wasn't anybody else on or near the lake."

Jack Stephens would like to know what caused this. If you know, or have an idea, he would like you to contact him at 937-692-5301.

20~Strange Earth Design in Michigan

A strange earth design covering 3 acres is reported to have been discovered in the early 1900s in Bruce Township.

According to Bela Hubbard's book, Memorials of a Half Century, a circular enclosure covering nearly 3 acres was found near the Clinton River in section 3 of Bruce Township. The report says that the circular earthen formation measured 450 by 400 feet. In it were 3 different openings or gates. Inside the circular enclosure near each of the openings or gates was a small mound of earth. In the nearby vicinity of the circular enclosure, 19 additional earthen mounds were found.

Hubbard also refers to mounds which were built of piled stone. The stones were piled to a height of 4 feet. The rock mounds are reported to have been discovered within a mile of the circular enclosure. It is said that skeletons were found under some of the rock piles. For more information on similar structures found in other parts of Michigan, see <u>Mystic Michigan Parts </u>1 and 3.

21~Michigan's Strange Rivers

In the Northern Hemisphere, most rivers flow towards the south. However, there seem to be several Michigan rivers that flow in the opposite direction. The St. Joseph River meanders through South Bend, Indiana, and then turns and flows north. It continues to flow north through Niles, Michigan, on its way to St. Joseph. The river runs past the ruins of an old fort that was built in the 1700s. The National Canoe and Kayak Association recognizes the river's oddity. It has held its last two national meetings in St. Joseph, Michigan.

This is not the only river that exhibits this strange behavior in Michigan. One northern Michigan man claims that he has seen a river in Michigan's Upper Peninsula that looks like it runs uphill, defying the laws of gravity. He claims that it happens on a section of Yellow Dog River near Independence Lake. This has not been verified at this time. If you know more about this, we would like to hear from you.

22~Michigan's Underwater Roads

There are many scenic and beautiful drives that may be enjoyed in Michigan. However, there are several Michigan roads that you won't be traveling on anytime soon, unless of course you happen to own a submarine. The reason for this is that some of Michigan's roads are under water.

Such is the case in St. Joseph, Michigan. The city has maps which actually have three roads on them which are submerged under several feet of water. So you and your family won't be doing any sight-seeing or going for a Sunday drive in that area anytime soon.

Those with scuba gear may be interested in trying to find the roads, although by this time they may be buried in sand. The waters of that region have also buried a park area and an entire performing pavilion. The park area was used in the early 1900s and became submerged in 1948 when water levels rose due to natural water cycles.

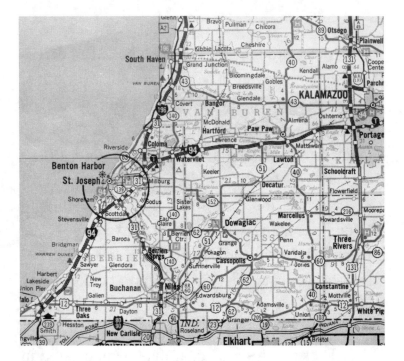

60

23~Will-o'-wisps of Michigan*

Darkness. A weary traveler wanders through the thick, vast wood of Michigan's primeval forest. He is lost, nervous...despairing. His courage ebbs as he ponders the possibility of passing in the night in an unfamiliar wood. Then he sees a light flitting through the branches somewhere in the distance. A lantern? Hope propels him on as he works his way through the impossibly dense underbrush toward the light. Just as the light seemingly comes within reach, he stumbles into a miry bog. Another unwary traveler has fallen victim to the tricks of the jack-o'-lantern.

Tales of the jack-o'-lantern and the will-o'-wisp have frightened the Michiganders from the state's earliest days. Today we know both phenomena as species of ignis fatuus. As organic matter decomposes in marshy ground, it can combust and give off eerie, phosphorescent lights. The slight heat generated by the rotting vegetation produces the shimmering effect of the will-o-wisp.

More rear are the glowing orbs of the jack-o'-lantern which bounce from tussock to tussock, sometimes breaking into smaller motes before finally dissipating. The movements of the jack-o'-lantern are still vaguely understood but some report that they occasionally accelerate when approaching human beings, giving the scared observer the impression of being chased.

European's transferred their superstitions surrounding marsh gases to Michigan as early as the mid-17th century, when French raconteurs warned their audiences to the sinister feu follet. The feu follet, they said, would magically lure nighttime travelers into boggy swamps or down steep chasms. To avoid succumbing to the blandishments of the feu follet, the raconteurs advised their listeners to hide and cover themselves until the evil passed. If the feu follet appeared near the home, one must immediately shut the house up or risk death by strangulation. In the area around Mackinac orbs of light were also considered omens. Two orbs seen at twilight were thought to be other-worldly signs of good fortune: a single orb, however, could only bode ill. French oral traditions continued in Michigan up to the time of statehood. Later European settlers perpetuated and amplified the folklore. Throughout the 19th century the Irish brought with them the shanachie's tales of the faerie lights, and Polish farmers making homes for themselves in southeastern Michigan added new elements to the legends. All traditions agreed that those walking at night would do best to ignore the dancing lights of the woodlands. As Michiganders gradually became a less rural and agricultural people in the 20th century, fascination with will-o'-wisps and jack-o'-lanterns waned. Those who still worked close to the earth, through, still saw strange lights in the thick, dark woods.

So it was one evening in 1989 for a small group of men descended from Michigan's 17th century habitants. Three generations of the de la Foret family gathered near Bellevue, in southwest corner of Eaton County-an are where the Potawatomi once feared the marshland as the home of the disease-bearing Fever Manitou. There, the three men were examining a site prior to cleaning it for development when they encountered a jack-o'-lantern. While the de la Fort's were looking over the wooded lot, a softball size orb of red light floated toward them, briefly hovered at a distance of 10 feet, and then quickly floated away-all the while never losing the intensify of it's glow. None of the men report ever having seen a similar object before or since.

24~Michigan's House of David

In days of old, various groups of religious people came to Michigan looking for a utopia. One such group was an assembly who called themselves the "House of David." They came to Michigan hoping to usher in the 1000-year reign of the Messiah on earth.

Most of the members wore long hair and beards and believed that they were a part of the regathering of Israel. Some of them believed that they were the descendants of the Jewish race. They built incredible buildings that resembled castles in Benton Harbor, Michigan. The architecture is classy, and the wealth it must have taken to build such buildings is staggering.

The need to build was so great that the members of the House of David actually bought an entire island with a mill on it to fill their needs. This island was called High Island. Their leader was a man named Benjamin Purnell. Some of the members of his communities called him King. The House of David still has a printing press where books can be purchased. If you are in the Benton Harbor area, the place is interesting to see.

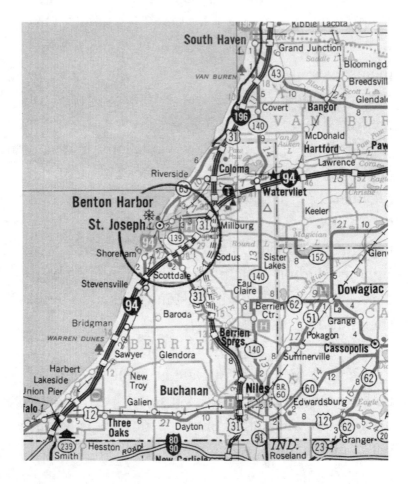

25~Michigan's Rock Face

Almost everyone has heard of the stone faces on Easter Island. However, it comes as a surprise to many people that there is a face carved in stone along a Lake Superior beach.

According to Marquette historian Fred Rydholm, there is a sculpted face staring out over Lake Superior at the east end of the Au Train beach. There are several different rumors as to who actually carved the formation. Rydholm states that credit for the sculpted face is disputed. One rumor about the face's origin is that it was carved by one of two different carvers in the 1920s. The other rumor is that it was carved by the Indians.

The rock face is depicted as staring solemnly out to Lake Superior. His lips are sealed, his outlook stern. He seems to be deep in thought, perhaps contemplating the legends of the lake as he looks out over the great inland sea. One can easily imagine that this face is patiently waiting for the arrival of a long lost mariner.

26~Michigan Island Treasure

Legends have persisted that vast treasures of Mormon gold are hidden on Beaver Island.

Rumors have been whispered for years that when a dissident sect of Mormons were expelled from Beaver Island by King James, they took their share of riches and buried them in Fox Lake on Beaver Island. The possibility of other treasures besides the treasures of Fox Lake have also been mentioned. A woman known as Mrs. Williams, author of the book <u>A Child of the Sea</u>, wrote, "The place they (the Mormons) chose to secrete their stolen goods was a long point at the lower end of Beaver Island, distant about 3 miles from the harbor. They called this place Rocky Mountain Point."

Those visiting the island who enjoy treasure hunting or metal detecting may wish to pinpoint these two areas while exploring Beaver Island. There are also enjoyable camping, historic, shopping and archaeological areas on the island that may be investigated.

27~Michigan's Geometric Formations

There are incredible claims concerning the geometric formations found in Michigan and in other places around the world. If various researchers are correct, there is something more than meets the eye when it comes to these strange earthen structures found throughout the state.

James Marshall of Illinois has researched the formations for years, and has been quoted in several articles in the Chicago Tribune on the subject. Marshall claims that the formations are connected mathematically over vast distances of thousands of miles.

Bonnie Gaunt of Jackson, Michigan, is a mathematician and archaeologist. She claims that the earthen structures in Michigan and other parts of the world may be ancient Hebrew monuments which contain mathematical information in their measurements relating to the second coming of the Hebrew Messiah.

Raymond Capt, a Biblical archaeologist who has studied the Great Pyramid and other archaeological structures throughout the world, also believes that the structures may have been built by some of the descendants of the sons of Noah who, he says, migrated here after the Flood.

There are a vast number of other researchers who believe that the structures were built by either the Adeena or Hopewell Indians. There are many different opinions concerning the origin of these ancient monuments found in Michigan. What do you think?

28~Michigan's Ancient Underwater Structure

Hundreds of feet out in Lake Huron lies what may be an ancient but not forgotten ruin.

Gary Nelkie of East Tawas thinks that there may be a man-made structure near Alpena in the waters of Thunder Bay. The giant rock formation is about 2 miles from shore on a huge shoal in about 2 feet of water. Nelkie believes the structure may have been an ancient fish trap built by Native Americans. He bases this idea on an experience he and another person had while they were out kayaking on Thunder Bay.

"While kayaking, we noticed that a large school of fish was following us. We paddled into the mouth of the rock formation. The fish followed us into the rock cove and became trapped inside. It seems to me that this is what the structure was made for." Native Americans had many brilliant ways of gathering food.

There may be other structures like the rock

formation in Alpena in various areas of the Great Lakes. The area that this structure is located in is near two islands which are natural wild-life refuge areas. It is against the law to trespass on them.

29~ Michigan's Meteorite Islands

There are actually several islands in Lake Superior that were formed by an asteroid.

According to the book <u>Mysterious Islands</u> by Andre Gooch, scientists have reported that a 19-mile-wide meteorite hit the Slate Island area thousands of years ago. The cluster of islands is reported to be what is left of the central cone from the original impact crater. On the island, there are dramatic cliffs and interesting rock formations which contain unique coloring and patterns. The Slate Islands in Lake Superior have been investigated by scientists on at least two separate occasions.

There have been many meteorite impacts in Michigan (see <u>Mystic Michigan </u>Part 1). The most recent that has come to our attention was the impact near Cadillac in 1999. The crash was reported by the Cadillac Evening News. Tim DeZeeuw of McBain, Michigan, claims to have heard explosions when the meteorite crashed. "I heard an explosion off in the distance at about the same time the news later reported that the meteorite had crashed," he said. DeZeeuw also reported that he had heard dishes rattling in the cupboard and windows vibrating in their frames when the strike took place.

1 Michigan's Ruins of Rome.............................Baldwin Historical Soc.
2 Michigan Mystic Tower
        Presque Isle Historical Soc................................ 517-734-4121
3 The Michigan Mermaid
        Sammy's Gift Store..517-362-6691
4 Michigan: Ancient Cemetery
5 Michigan's 1999 Fireball Phenomenon
        Cadillac News Paper, 1999 Archives................231-775-6565
6 Michigan's Subterranean World......................www.detroitsalt.com
7 Michigan's Hemlock Lights
8 Michigan Treasure Island Hermit
9   Strange Animal Encounters in Mich
10 Lake Erie's Carry Grotto
        Perry's Cave 419-285-2405, Crystal Cave 419-285-2811
11 Michigan's Underwater Forest
12 Michigan's Circle and Square
        Hinsdales Archaeological Atlas of Michigan
13 The Lights of Michigan's Denton Rd.
        Detroit Free Press 1999 Archives
14 Michigan's Reappearing Historic Ship
        Archadia Historical Soc. 231-889-4360
15 Michigan's Forest Cemeteries
16 Michigan's Lost Gold Mine
17 Michigan's Underwater Metropolis
18 Medieval Michigan
19 Michigan Explosion Oddity
20 Strange Earth Design in Michigan.
        Hinsdales Archeological Atlas of Michigan
21 Michigan's Strange Rivers
22 Michigan's Underwater Roads
23 Michigan's Will-o'-wisp
24 Michigan's House of David.....................................616-926-6695
25 Michigan's Rock Face.........Superior Heart Land by Fred Rydholm
26 Michigan Island Treasure....................Beaver Island Historical Soc.
27 Michigan's Geometric Formations
        Hinsdale's Archeological Atlas of Michigan
28 Michigan's Ancient Underwater Structure
29 Michigan's Meteorite Islands

The numbers identified with each article in this book represent it's location on the map below and information for further research listed on the previous page.

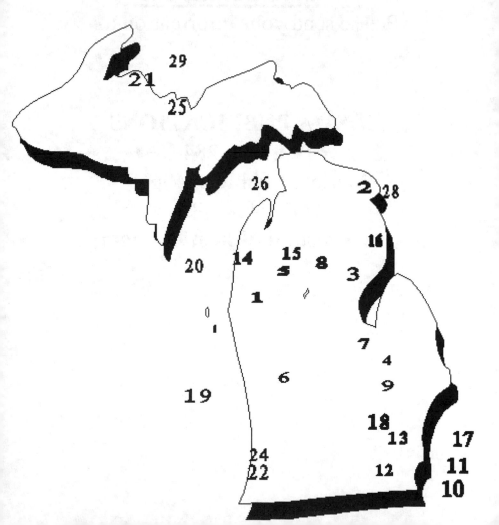

If you have an unusual fact or phenomenon about the great state of Michigan or about an odd Michigander and would like to see your story in a future edition of

<u>Mystic Michigan</u>

Please send your information to:

ZOSMA PUBLICATIONS
P.O. Box 284
Marion, Michigan 49665
231-743-6984
www.zosmapublications.com